Published by Spadge UK

Cover illustrated by Rosie Rockets | Cover & content designed by Rick Nunn

ISBN: 978-0-9934299-1-0

For my mother, my muse.

My love is undeterred by your higher Twitter following.

Huge Love/
♡ 3
← Spadge
xo

INTRODUCTION

There are two types of women in this world. The first is the type of woman whose mother is insanely proud of everything they do. The second is the type of woman serving a prison sentence for murdering their mother in cold blood, and disposing of her body in a manner that wouldn't even vaguely meet her domesticated standards.

Which one am I? I find, like most women, that it varies depending on my hunger level.

I should, in no way, be classed as a role model for fellow women. My cooking and driving skills are abysmal, I loathe house chores, I eat with my fingers and I swear like Danny Dyer at a football match. However, I also have a healthy makeup addiction, love a cocktail, carry my Chihuahua around in a handbag and enjoy that yearly panic where I feel the need to completely change my hairstyle for no good reason. When it comes to femininity, I'd say I'm a close 50/50, by which I mean my legs are shaved for about half of the year.

I know that many female friends feel the same way and so I hoped that, under the bulletproof armour of anonymity, I could coax some very interesting stories out of them, perhaps even picking up some handy tips along the way. How does one stabilize kitchen fires, for example? Is there anything more painful than epilation? How many Cosmopolitans are too many Cosmopolitans? And so on and so forth.

What inspired this book:

After a brief flirtation with sociology, I discovered that there was, in existence, a series of books from the 1850s titled "Manners". These books were used as a kind of 'how to' guide, encouraging people of the 19th Century to behave in a more civilised manner. "Blow your nose into handkerchiefs instead of onto your neighbour's sleeve", "Stop defecating wildly around the kitchen", etcetera. I'm paraphrasing. However, this made me realise that there was actually a time where blowing your nose into your fingers was a normal thing to do. I don't know about you, but I think some people haven't realised that times have changed and that they have yet to catch up with the modern world.

I should probably invest in a handkerchief.

I find that people of older generations particularly, such as parents and grandparents, still expect us to follow the same rules as they did, and make us feel like subhuman imbeciles if we disclose our own methods. We are so often advised on the best ways to cook, shop, clean, drive and socialise. "You're using that brand of gravy?" "Don't throw it out, just patch it up for the fifth time." "Watch out for that pedestrian!" Nazis. We're taught what not to say, what not to do, we're taught to avoid eye contact with strange men (which only aggravates them more, trust me) and we're taught to be feminine throughout the entirety of these tasks. When my Grandma was at school she wasn't "supposed to" eat in the street and so it always surprises her when I tuck into a packet of crisps while we wander about town. "Sarah-Jean, put those away, you're getting salt all down your far-too-visible cleavage". Seriously, if I couldn't eat in the street then most days I'd never find time for lunch at all.

My mother is a very good example of a traditional house-wife and by that I mean that if she goes away for a week-end, the house falls apart without her. She does at least one load of washing every single day and always used to have a packed lunch ready on the table for everyone before work and school. This wasn't due to boredom, trust me, she's still far busier than I am, yet somehow I can't find the time to even grab myself a Pot Noodle on my way out of the door. My lifestyle seems to surprise older generations; I work around my own schedule, I'm covered in tattoos, I'm (currently) living a mortgage-free life with a husband that I lived with for years before marrying him and I constantly divulge unladylike information in public places. I consider myself an absolute delight, yet I seem to embarrass other people.

I genuinely think it's OK that we don't have our lives as organised as our parents did at our age, and I revel in the daily rebellion of never ironing my underwear. I know our generation loves to complain, check what's trending on Twitter and you'll see my point, but we have it pretty easy really. I read about how difficult women had it in previous decades and I don't think I'd trade. I love that we can vote and get our legs out in public, right up to our bum cheeks, judging by the fourteen year olds in Primark, but there's more of a public eye on women than ever before. And with that newfound judgement, comes a whole ton of never-before-felt pressure – any culinary failure is imme-diately followed by a friend posting a picture of their own masterpiece and, if by some miracle, you cook something that you're proud of, a bunch of other people will instantly inform you about how incorrect you are. Family members will tag you in life-ruining photos and an innocent photo of your dog doing something cute will reveal the pigsty that is your house in the background. Social media is a landmine of public failure and embarrassment.

Women must be well-groomed, career-driven, competitive, yet modest, funny, sexy, gym-going, healthy-eating, outgoing, hiding their IBS symptoms, having babies at just the right time and above all, managing it all without having a public breakdown in IKEA. Plus, at any given moment, at least three of your friends will be doing any of the above far better than you. If you have children as well as HD Brows, you are legitimately my new real life superhero and I will stalk you until I am arrested for perversion. My best friend in the whole world recently had a baby and walked around with only one waxed armpit for eight days. Eight days. That, my friend, is a real modern-mother. The rest of you are doing it wrong.

My point is, despite what you see on social media, television and in magazines, you're doing OK. Sure, in my dreams I'm the kind of woman who has the time to make homemade scones at the weekend or who could, in fact, make anything homemade that didn't involve putting shampoo and conditioner in my hand at the same time, but alas, my scones make for far better weaponry than anything remotely edible or sanitary.

I was absolutely certain that I wasn't alone in this daily trek through a minefield of domestic masquerade. I decided that this book will become that proof. Anybody that I lightly (heavily) interrogated about the subject of 'being a modern woman' lit up with passion, as if I had stoked the flame within an internal feministic fire pit (usually a UTI). I soon discovered that many women were sat in the same boat as me, clutching a 'Spadge, relate to me!' lifejacket for dear life, while Snapchatting a selfie from an angle that hides the Marmite in their freshly-bleached moustache.

So, before this boatload of Megababes goes down, here are some truths that we've kept to ourselves for far too long...

Anonymous Modern Women, I can't thank you enough for sharing your stories.

All quotes inside this book came from real women.

30 real women aged between 20 and 35, and all of whom made the excellent decision to be friends with me on Facebook.

CONTENTS:

Chapter One:

CLOTHING

(shopping)

Dressing yourself is hard. And not just physically. I mean, trying to fit into new snug jeans is never easy, but getting them off again is damn right near impossible. Ankles are generally smaller in diameter than feet, which makes skinny jeans a terrible, relationship-ruining invention. I often just sleep in them and hope nobody notices how long I've been trapped inside them. Have you ever worn skinny jeans on a date that starts to go particularly well? Dreadful isn't it. You start to panic-sweat when they invite you in after the meal which, surprisingly, doesn't help to loosen them. You're picturing doing the dreadfully unsexy, hopping-around flamingo dance while wobbling about all over their bedroom, trying to get your tiny trouser hem over your supposedly normal-sized foot. Damn you, H&M, you're making my feet look like flippers in front of the lovely man who thinks the dinner he just ever-so-kindly paid for has gone straight to my left foot.

Whenever I enter a clothes shop, I feel like I am never dressed well enough. I feel that the people who work there are going to be like "Damn, I can see you really need our help, drastically, but I really don't want to be seen talking to you right now." People inside these places are naturally going to be at least a mild fan of clothing and fashion, and I just don't know how to talk to these people. It comes across as sarcastic every time: "Hi there, could you please point me in the direction of the section where the clothing isn't made from plastic fur?" just leave Spadge, just leave.

Occasionally, I will find a selection of clothing that I think looks pretty good on the rack (or mannequin, which I closely resemble in both ghostly complexion and enthusiasm for being in the shop), yet when I get them to the dressing room, everything is all wrong. There's just so much pressure not to get it wrong. Did you know that wearing an "offensive" T-shirt is a criminal offence under Section 5 of the Public Order Act in the UK? Yep. £80 fine, on the spot, I kid you not. I know what you're thinking: (1.) How ridiculous! And (2.) How ever will I spot my hilarious soulmate in the street now? (Tinder, mate. Hilarious bios are the new hilarious T-shirt slogans). I, myself, am a bit of a rebel in regards to this Public Order Act law. I have a risque love heart tattooed on my ankle. It sounds innocent, I know, but when I'm wearing just the right length of sock, then the top half of the heart looks a bit like a pair of testicles sticking out of the top. You can tell how badass I'm feeling by the length of my trousers some days.

I'm at the age, late twenties, where I now look for practicality alongside style, a very difficult combination to find. Comfortable shoes are particularly essential where I live because I often have to run from children with knifes, or from police who have spotted the testicle-heart tattoo on my ankle. But at least I will never, ever, opt for leggings instead of trousers. Am I right ladies?

"

*I once spent a good 30 minutes plus in a changing room
watching an episode on Netflix to find out if the dress I
was trying on was remotely like one of the characters to
find out my headphone jack wasn't in properly and the
whole changing room area heard both the programme and
myself in hysterics laughing.*

"

"

For my 18th, my mum took me to Amsterdam. We spent a few hours in "cafés", wandered through the red light district, then on to the main shopping centre. I tried on a few clothes, but didn't buy anything. Only when I got home did I realise I'd accidentally stolen some clothes and put my clothes on over the top.

"

"

So one morning, utterly hungover, I begrudgingly got dressed for my 11am shift at work at a local bar and headed into town. My short walk to work was about ten minutes along the busy main road through the town centre. I stepped outside the front door into unexpected blinding sunlight. Fumbling for my sunglasses to relieve to my already post alcohol afflicted pupils, I covered my face with Paris Hilton-esque bug eyes (circa 2008) and made my slow commute on foot. Now about 5 minutes into my journey I noted how exceptionally bright the sun was on this morning. I mean really bright, so bright it hurt. And this was WITH sunglasses on.

I concluded my current physical & mental state was to blame. Perhaps the excessive intake of "treble trebles" and my obsession with The Twilight Saga was taking its toll.

I also shook off the feeling people were eyeing me strangely, put my head down and walked on.

It wasn't until almost completing my journey to work, upon reaching the glass doors to the bar I happened upon my reflection...

I had been so painfully absorbed in my hangover, I had failed to realise that I was missing a lens to my sunglasses.

That's right, like Lindsey Lohan playing smelly pirate hooker, I had stumbled my way into town with one black bug eye, and one empty lens, like it was totally normal.

To this day when wearing sunglasses I get flashbacks, and can be seen frequently touching the lenses to make sure they are still there.

"

"

I once had a coat that I looked awesome in. So this day I peel myself out of bed, dress up nice, put the coat and a pair of gorgeous heels on and strut out of my student digs channeling Beyoncé (as you do) to suddenly having this lovely young woman running up behind me shouting "miss! Miss! You er...." and handing me a pair of dirty knickers that had got tangled up on my heel. I was mortified, as was she when she realised. I went straight into town and bought a laundry basket. Didn't leave my room for days in case I bumped into her.

"

"

I think my worst moment was when I wore a thong the wrong way round for an entire day. It had felt uncomfortable, but I figured that was pretty standard for a thong... but later on when I was undressing I discovered that not only was it inside out, but the crotch area was on my hip. I haven't really worn one since.

"

"

When leggings were the 'in thing' I lived in them, who wouldn't - so comfy after a pair of jeans! I had worn them quite often for a while before realising they were see through, so half the city did see my knickers on a day to day basis. You'd think this would stop me from wearing them, no - pure comfort won over my dignity!

"

"

I'm completely against shoplifting, but I once shoplifted with my sister, on New Year's day, just for the thrill of it.

"

"

I'm not allowed to shop online after 6pm, my sense of sensibility goes out the window and I will buy everything when I don't have the money to do so. I quite often ignore this and do it anyway...and then can't sleep very well out of guilt. I get over it when I feel fabulous in my new buys.

"

"

Okay I'm not a very good dresser from a fashion perspective, but I usually manage to at least put the right shoe on the right foot. I did however go to an adult play centre (as in inflatable obstacle courses and climbing nets, not whips and chains) not so long ago and, in my enthusiasm, I did manage to split my jeans - and spent the rest of the time sitting sadly in a ball pit.

"

Chapter Two:

GROOMING

(bleaching)

There is a very general and well-known rule that women are expected to be well-groomed at all times. It's important for me that you understand that these are expectations I like to follow very closely myself. I feel most comfortable when I'm bristle-free and not having to subtly scratch myself in the Post Office queue. At the same time, there is absolutely no judgement from me if you prefer the warmer look, I quite envy the time you must save, but my point is that there isn't a man telling me I have to sleep in full makeup (in fact the complete opposite is true - the one time I slept in waterproof eyeliner, he got really mad about the permanent panda-face marks on the new white pillowcase). I'm fully pro-choice. Pro-groom or no-groom, I'll hug anyone if they buy me a Mars bar.

I think that my crazy low self esteem comes from years of unachievable media expectations, but this seems to have increased dramatically since I acquired a HD 4K television last year. Where are the pores on these women?! My own complexion seems to more often resemble the baby animals on Springwatch, instead of any of the humans presenting the show, with possibly the exception of Bill Oddie.

Actresses seem to have zero facial hair though, right? Even in close-ups, in unflattering light. Not even the tiniest bleached remnants of a moustache. To the relaxed eye, and in direct light, their top lip looks immaculate, but if I stand with the light behind me, my above-the-lip hairs are illuminated like a beacon telling the world that I'm less evolved than other women. Seriously, my face looks twice as wide when you take the fair hairs into consideration.

I remember the first time I ever noticed the micro-hairs on my face. Have you ever been browsing a huge department store like IKEA and stumbled across those mirrors with the five-time zoom? I wrapped my long (head) hair all the way around my face for the rest of the shopping trip, because that seemed like the less-hairy option. I have actually considered shaving my face before, but then I worry that I'll get the same rash as I do under my arms, and that would be even more embarrassing than a slightly hairy chin. People see a rash around your mouth and the mind jumps straight to Herpes. Just me?

Grooming starts at such a young age, it seems most of us became paranoid about these things at school. You'd think we would be used to the routines by now? Well I, for one, like to see what I can "get away with" as the years go by. I think I am becoming more cunning, or perhaps just less embarrassed? I'm definitely less bothered about answering the door to the postman while my moustache bleach is still setting in, for example, but I have also become very skilled at learning the days I probably won't have to reveal my legs to anyone. The fast-shower days. If you're ever feeling guilty about skipping a wax session or a shave day, then feel free to borrow my mantra of an excuse:

Forms of hair removal may have been practiced since 10,200 BC, but those were days long before the very distracting and addictive invention of Netflix.

"

*Every month I have to tweeze this one solitary beard hair
out my chin…*

"

"

I once had my face waxed and drove home looking like I'd been repeatedly slapped with a wet fish.

"

"

As part of my job, I was doing an intimate bikini wax on a lady who wanted the whole thing off. Half way through whilst I was applying the strip and rubbing it on so it was stuck properly, I accidentally slipped one up her, just a quick in and out...

"

"

I have PCOS (Polycystic Ovary Syndrome) which means my body is an absolute WONDERLAND. This means I have a regular routine that involves shaving my beard (a delicate procedure), plucking my chin, and occasionally shaving my hobbit feet. I'm not in the least bit ashamed about this (body hair just kind of does its own thing) but it does take some time and effort. I sometimes feel I should grow it all out - I've always been fond of the Addams Family.

"

"

I have a hair that grows out of a mole that my ex nick-named Spike.

"

"

I once thought I'd try Veet on my upper lip in attempt to get rid of a 'miss-tache' (annoying dark haired genes) - left it on too long, hair was removed, but I then had a bright red and very sore moustache for the next 12 hours instead.

"

"

I once needed some deodorant desperately in an emergency but couldn't find any, so I had to use bathroom air freshener!

"

"

I regularly use my husband's beard trimmer to keep 'downstairs' tidy - I'm sure he wouldn't mind haha!

"

"

*I spend far too long covering up my freckles with founda-tion just to draw them back on again with a brown pencil.
I blame beauty standards.*

"

"

I was getting a pedicure and the lady asked if I would like the hair on my toes waxing, or braiding :-(

,,

Chapter Three:

Communicating

(swearing)

Note:

This chapter contains swear words.

I hope you are not offended by this. People are offended by all sorts of pissing shit these days.

Women are expert communicators. It's a fact. They can have entire conversations using just their eyes, even in the darkest and busiest of rooms. With their words, they can make waiters resign on the spot for bringing them the wrong drink and with the right amount of dedication, they can even trick men (who are very against marriage) into marrying them. Husband, if you're reading this, this is a test to see how far into this book you've read.

Seriously though, women are scientifically better communicators than men. Evidence from a study by Marlene LeFever shows that female babies are born with a more acute sense of hearing and brains which are more finely developed, giving us the ability to read and react to situations much faster than males. Which makes me an absolute mystery to science. Not joking. Even when someone gives me clear, straightforward instruction, I can become totally baffled by what I should be doing. It's possible that I became distracted by an attractive window cleaner or, you know, dust. I am pretty good, however, at using female eyebrow code; I can simply turn and raise one eyebrow in the direction of a female friend and she smiles in full, juicy acknowledgement of my subtextual statement.

I love watching men become confused by this. "Why are you laughing? What did she just say to you with that eyebrow raise?" "That you're a bellend." I do also love a good swear. Swearing is one of my favourite ways to communicate. Nothing shows enthusiasm like a swear word. I truly believe that these words show passion, that they show anger, that they show a kind of ecstaticness that is so fucking ecstatic that there are simply no other words to use to better describe it. For example, I often call my best friends "hot bitches" or "fucking bellends", because I'm so full and overcome with love that I get a bit aggressive.

The guys at my local Subway are fine with my colourful gratitude every time they hand me a delicious sandwich. But as soon as someone else in the queue announces "swearing is so unladylike", all the female eyebrows go up. Bellend. I fully understand that there is a time and a place, but there are certain moments in life when even the most ladylike of ladies will need to delve into the darker areas of her vocabulary... "YES! you summed up that situation perfectly, you sexy eloquent bitch".

Hearing other women swear or fumble with their communication, particularly if accidentally, will always make me smile. May these communication mishaps continue to surprise the shit out of us all...

"

I once said 'package' about 5 times whilst delivering a lecture to 200 people. I then brought attention to it by saying 'sorry I have no idea why I keep saying package'.

"

"

I once asked for chicken niggets at the McDonald's drive thru. You're reading that correctly.

"

"

I was writing a shopping list whilst calling a client and when he answered I said "Hello, can I speak to Mr Femfresh please?"

"

"

It was ridiculously hot at my place of work and the only way to keep cool was to wear as little as possible, so I opted for loose fitting dresses. As per usual, I was wearing said dress type one day, but I hadn't done my washing that week and was very low on underwear. Now when you're travelling, there's always going to be a pair of pants that aren't quite up to scratch. They're the pair of grey ones (useful under light clothing), but haven't quite stood up to the harsh washing machines of the hostels, so the material is very thin and may have a few holes here and there, basically very grim and not at all sexy.

I had to wear those particular pants this day…this every so slightly windy day. And as I walked out of work, of course my dress flew up over my head, in front of a very good looking customer all the counter girls fancied and after my very loud exclamation, 'OH SHIT BALLS!'. Mr Hotness laughed and told everyone I had showed him my secrets. Mortified.

"

"

In every interview or important meeting, I have to fight the yawning. I think it's a nervous thing but I worry by trying to keep them in I look like I'm constipated.

"

"

I'm a big casual cunter, in an affectionate way. If I call you a cunt I probably like you.

"

"

I once was babysitting my ex's 8 year old brother. We were playing PlayStation and every time he beat me I said "bollocks" not meaning to of course, but also not thinking it was that bad of a swear word anyway! He said it later in front of the whole family to which I told him off! I felt so bad and confessed it was me but many years later!

"

"

I sometimes talk to myself. And when people look at me, I just pretend I have no idea what they are looking at.

"

"

Group texting - meaning to send a message to an individual about the group but you end up sending it to the group by mistake. I've done this in a work situation and said to the group (meaning to send to a friend) 'so annoyed with work right now, they're pathetic all of them'

die and call in sick

"

"

I once told my ex boyfriend that I was pregnant for April fools. He took it very seriously and came back at the end of the day with a 5 year plan depending on what decision we came to. At the time it wasn't funny but looking back it really is.

"

"

I grabbed a guy's head instead of the seat rail whilst getting off the bus once. We both just froze like that until the bus stopped and I made my hasty exit.

"

"

I like to use the word 'cunt' on a regular basis because I love how people squirm when they hear it, especially coming from a woman.

"

Chapter Four:

HOBBYING

(stalking)

Subjectively, I'd say that what we get up to in our spare time are probably some of the strangest confessions I've read. That's definitely what I was after here, I just wasn't entirely sure where to put these, so I'm just gonna leave them here in 'Hobbying'. (I mostly like to make up new words in my spare time.)

From literal stalking, to fictional music video making and mastering celebrity walks, I feel both inspired and a little bit scared for your partner's exes. Stay weird, guys. Stay weird.

"

I watch Food Network in spite of the fact that I've seen literally every episode of every show at least twice. I like to play Nigella Lawson sexy bingo, which basically involves staring at my partner like I'm on The Office every time Nigella says something like "of course, my mouth can accommodate" or "it's all part of the pleasure". A great game, which I would highly recommend!

"

"

I like to read comment sections that make me angry into the wee hours, and then watch kitten videos to calm me down.

"

"

Sometimes I look out the window and pretend I'm in a dramatic music video. It helps if it's raining.

"

"

I live my life thinking I'm in the Truman show, but knowing I know I'm in the Truman show so I narrate and sing everything I do.

"

"

I watch my cats sleep.

"

"

In my spare time I am a bugger for major Facebook/Instagram stalking of exes and their partners, or just people who I am intrigued by. Facebook doesn't show much unless you are their friend, and I am incredibly disappointed when someone's Instagram profile is private. However, when it isn't, I go to town for a good half hour or so!

"

"

I'm obsessed with a YouTuber and spent around 30 mins finding her flat on Zoopla.

"

"

I love popping spots even though I shouldn't.

"

"

I go around beauty departments in search of a free "fuss" (the free fuss is better than the kind of fusses you pay for) I'm so bad that I've had to move my radius wider because everyone knows I'm just there to get touched on the face by a stranger and I have absolutely no intention of buying anything. I once got a "Unicorn Healing" from a lady who swung a big crystal in my face for 25 minutes and held my shoulders and it was the best feeling in the world, until she told me I owed her £25.

"

"

*I watch Gossip Girl and Sex and the City consistently.
Few days go by where I don't walk (or skip) about thinking I have a Carrie Bradshaw swag or fantasise about
Chuck Bass picking me up in his limo.*

"

"

Me and my best friend once got stuck in a pretzel shape with each other and laughed so hard that we both needed to pee, urgently. We realised we were a little too far away from the toilet to make it, so we made a pact to both piss ourselves, together. In solidarity, after 3.

Friend - "One, two, Th- Actually I think I can hold it now" *runs to the toilet*

Me - "Wait, what"

I had to walk around all day covered in my own pee.

"

Chapter Five:

Relaxing

(pooping)

Does anyone else find relaxing situations stressful, or is it just me? Last year I conquered some of my biggest fears, including flying, spiders and public speaking, so it was suggested to me "Why don't you try and have a really relaxing year this year?" Honestly, trying to relax is definitely one of the most stressful things I could do. Take, for example, a short spa day. That day involves being naked at certain points, frequently make-up less and you're touched repeatedly by strangers (professionals, I might add). How is that relaxing? Why do you think they give you a glass of Prosecco upon arrival? Relaxation is all a big ruse.

I find any kind of day event stressful to be honest, and there is one specific reason why. During that day there is a completely natural, but extremely shameful thing, that I will absolutely have to do. No matter where I am or what I'm busy doing, I'm going to have to poop at some point. And that poop is going to have to be performed with the skilled subtlety of a toilet ninja. Even when I'm in a huge public toilet, the place you should feel most inclined to relieve yourself in, I have to fashion a toilet-paper type of net, in an attempt to mask the evident plop sound that would otherwise follow. Why is there so much stigma around women defecating these days? I'm pretty sure the Romans used to all poo in a line on the same toilet-bench. Let's bring back that social activity?!

I have very healthy bowels at the best of times. And, if you listen closely, you can hear the sound of my grandma dying of shame. But so many activities make me need the toilet faster than usual. Exercise? Can we stop, I gotta poop. Coffee date? Definitely gonna have to poop. Food date? You're literally feeding my need to poop. It's something I fret about constantly.

I promised you nothing if not useful advice in this book, but I would recommend not reading this chapter while eating or, if you're a sympathetic pooer like I am, maybe don't read this on a train, where the bathroom facilities are far less than preferable.

To sum up, let's all be more open about what actually helps us relax. Talk to me about your woes, or invite me to a poo bench party and we'll be friends for life…

"

*The hairdressers is an extremely stressful place. Sometimes
I write a list of possible topics for conversation.... Xfactor,
Great British Bake Off, Are you going out tonight?
Holiday plans?*

"

"

I get so stressed out by the very idea of booking a holiday. How do you do that? How do you know what's good value? How do you choose a resort?

IT IS MEANT TO BE RELAXING, SOMEONE ELSE DO THIS FOR ME.

"

"

When doing any group activities (i.e. wine tours) I panic about someone wanting to start a conversation and mess up my fun.

,,

"

When guided to 'breathe naturally' in meditation I forget how, in regards to both frequency and volume.

"

"

I never enjoy a meal out, I always worry I'll get sick.

"

"

I barely drink when I'm out so I don't have to use public bathrooms or have to go into a place to ask to use the loo in case they say no. If I'm desperate, I'll pretend to be pregnant so they can't refuse me.

"

"

I get so excited about going to sleep that I stress myself out and can't sleep.

"

"

I go into panic mode if I ever use a toilet that has no soap - that is definitely one of my worst nightmares. I also don't trust anyone who never washes their hands after going to the toilet. Those people are the reason I can't bring myself to touch door handles.

"

"

I'm rather self conscious about my body, so sunbathing and going to the beach or swimming pool is a real stress for me. I will accidentally on purpose forget my swimmers or cover up as much as I can without looking like a right idiot. I plan what to wear very carefully. I think a lot of people feel like this though. We all just have to remember we don't really judge what other people look like at the beach or pool, whether they're big or small, so why would anyone care about us? I'm getting a bit better with this.

"

"

I had a massage in Seychelles and the masseuse kept farting. It made me more tense and he offered me an extra half hour for free because my "muscles need it"!

"

"

I worry about people seeing my phone because I'm always bitching about someone over messenger.

"

"

I always think I like having massages but whenever I do they are so painful. Why can you never build up the courage to tell them they're hurting you. Then when you come out, you're always more tense than when you went in.

"

"

Going to the beach - you have to go through the whole de-hairing, what to wear, what to take with you, is it acceptable to take a mini suitcase across sand dunes? How to act when you're getting changed on the beach as everyone stares at you. Taking lessons from a contortionist to get your body in certain positions so when you put your sun cream on you avoid rolls of fat being visible. Worrying you should wear footwear in the sea as to not get attacked by sea monsters (also better grip for running out of the sea) the list is endless…

"

"

I have an overactive imagination, things always seem worse in my head. If I hear a floorboard creak I'm convinced after 5 minutes of overthinking that I'm going through the floor.

"

"

I have a mole on the back of my head and every single time a hairdresser touches my head, all I can think about is "Don't touch my mole, don't touch my mole".

"

Chapter Six:

COOKING

(microwaving)

Although I'm no connoisseur in the kitchen, there is one dish that I have absolutely mastered. I say dish… it's more often a mug, because then it microwaves faster. But does that stop me trying to cook more exotic dishes? No. Should it? Probably, but I'm not one to be deterred by confusing spoon sizes, aggressive pan fires or severe bouts of food poisoning.

There are some major factors that affect my ability to cook and eat well. Time is a major one for me, not just the time spent preparing and cooking the food, but planning around the unnecessary complications of best-before dates. Fruit and vegetables are the worst for this. What do they have, like, one day of shelf life? Even when you stock your fridge right up with goodies, everything seems to go out of date at the same time and you end up eating the weirdest combination of things. "Spadge, is there avocado in this lasagna or something?". Okay, that's a terrible example because that sounds delicious, avocado is some kind of magical cheese-like fruit, but you catch my drift. It's the same whenever I feel like baking. Maybe I'll feel like making myself some gooey cookies for dessert (breakfast), only to find that the flour went out of date two years ago and while I'm at the corner shop, I'll simply buy instant cookies instead of putting flour back into the pointless-storage cycle. Send me all the recipes you like, I'll always choose either what's fastest to cook or what is going out of date first.

'Eating' is something else that comes into play here, it's a skill not quite as tricky as cooking, but I've found it is met with similar guilt if completed to a low standard. With a lack of cooking ability comes a lot of takeaways. And I must say, reading the confessions in this chapter made me feel a whole lot better about the amount of takeaway bags I hide from my husband. I destroy any evidence that suggests how bad I am at fending for myself.

Cooking was never a skill that I was taught when growing up, I find no joy in it at all. In fact, I remember specifically being told that baking and cooking made too much mess in the kitchen, so it wasn't really allowed at home. Why don't they put more emphasis on these things at school; cooking and eating well? Eating is a basic necessity for survival, along with calculating taxes and returning slightly soiled clothes to department stores after their final return date. I can't remember the last time I used Pythagoras, but I sure as hell remember eating that mouldy bagel last week… education is to blame here, for sure.

"

I once poured boiling water on pasta in the middle of the kitchen floor. My brain didn't register that the water needed somewhere to go.

"

"

Once I just ate a whole bag of hundreds and thousands.

,,

"

Cooking isn't so much of a problem for me as eating. I eat out of boredom, procrastination, sadness, illness, happiness … anything and I think I'm a little addicted to sugar. I'm not overweight, but I don't particularly enjoy exercise enough to not worry about it so it's a bit of battle. Some days I win, most I lose.

"

"

If my husband isn't in I just eat toast and biscuits instead of cooking.

"

"

My boyfriend was on a pretty intense military training course, I thought I'd be nice and make him & the other guys some chocolate brownies. I don't bake - 70% of them were burnt but I had invested so much time into them that I decided to give them to him anyway, letting him know that it was my thought that counted.

"

"

I was cooking chicken in my new oven, except I accidentally put it on 'grill' not 'fan'. There was smoke everywhere causing the fire alarm to go off which then sent an alert to security. Not my finest moment!

"

"

I sometimes have McDonalds and hide the bags from my partner.

"

"

I live on toast most of the time.

"

"

I set fire to my mother-in-law's kitchen, trying to boil eggs. Don't ask.

"

Chapter Seven:

CLEANING

(disguising)

I've inherited many fine traits from my mother, her humour, her face shape, her need to dance to every Madonna song ever, no matter the location or how familiar the company… why then, did I not inherit her extremely desirable tendency to clean?

For many, the taste of Sunny Delight and watching clouds float across a summer sky remind them of childhood, for me, it's the smell of Dettol.

I really dislike cleaning. It's not even the physical task of cleaning, more the concept behind it. I don't mind the hard work; the battle between vacuum and the edge of the damn curtains, or even removing day old, cold, wet food remnants from the drain in the sink. I'm not squeamish or a snob, I just think there are a million other things I'd rather be doing and trust me, I manage to find them.

This stalling technique is all well and good until someone announces they are going to drop by for a visit. Suddenly organising my flours by use-by date doesn't seem so important. I have to prioritise. What rooms are they likely to go in? I prepare to block their view of particularly cluttered areas with my body, I release the wild pigeons that have gathered around the washing up and then I spray a subtle stream of air freshener around doorways. It's all about creating an illusion, I become the David Copperfield of cleanliness, and you can too.

It's worth noting here, ladies, that about 25% of you admitted to being 'clean freaks'. If this thing wasn't anonymous, we could no longer be friends…

"

I pick my nose and flick it behind the bed. It's gross, my partner hates it, and she's named it 'Booger Mountain'.

"

"

When I went to my dad's place once every two weeks as a kid, I'd leave half a cup of tea in my room to see what sort of mouldy stuff would grow.

"

"

Sometimes I just leave the hoover out so it looks like cleaning is in progress… it's not.

"

"

It takes me 15 minutes or more cleaning up the sink and my hands alone once I've touched raw chicken :(Dettol spray lasts a week in our house.

"

"

I just sprayed air freshener so it smelt like I'd cleaned and then complained when my husband "messed" it up.

"

"

I was so against washing the dishes I would regularly eat cereal from a tumbler glass with a fork.

"

"

I ice skate around the kitchen floor on baby wipes because it's quicker than mopping.

"

"

In our first year of uni we used paper plates and cups so we didn't have to wash up. (We are terrible humans).

"

"

My housemate left butter in her kitchen cupboard while she went on holiday, I came back to bugs and maggots! As I was moving out the next few days I left it for her to clean up!

"

"

If I don't have time before people come over, I shove all the mess in the spare room.

"

"

I hate cleaning my teeth before bed, mainly due to laziness and wanting to get into bed the second I feel tired. I only do it when my boyfriend stays, just to keep up appearances.

"

"

I always wait until the washing basket is overflowing before I decide to wash my clothes, which means I sometimes have to spend a few days not wearing underwear.

"

"

I hate the feeling of wet teabags, so if a guest drinks tea I have to leave the bag in the sink until my husband gets rid of it for me.

"

"

My partner has to forcibly remove my socks from me because I will wear them for a week without flinching.

"

Chapter Eight:

Driving

(also swearing)

Legally, and physically, I cannot drive. I don't often use the word 'can't' (careful!), but I really can't. You would think this might put me off including this chapter, but you'd be wrong. I have witnessed enough valiant women behind the wheel to know exactly what to expect.

Let's lay down some statistics to really put gender into perspective when it comes to driving. Statistically, more men have experienced car crashes. More male drivers kill pedestrians, animals and themselves while operating a car. Men also, statistically, have become distracted more easily when driving, have been more aggressive when driving, and are twice as likely to speed. The number of men also doubles the number of women who have driven under the influence of drink or drugs. Hey, I'm not judging (I am), but there's a reason I don't drive and you guys are it. Nobody has the patience for my meticulous, anxiety-ridden manoeuvres.

Why do women get all of the stereotypical abuse? Don't get me wrong, I once blocked a busy yellow box junction, I have stalled mid-roundabout and I have crashed my dad's brand new Golf GTI into the gate of his driveway. But I have also witnessed female friends drive at least four miles off route to avoid crossing a scary dual carriageway, and I saw another have a panic attack when they couldn't do a hill start in front of a Porsche. If that's not taking safety to a new, deeply emotional level, then I don't know what is.

Some female drivers I know are fearless, badass and highly enjoy driving, but most of them (myself included) hate it with a passion.

Remember, the human body was never built to withstand speeds of more than four miles per hour, so anything you do over that is fucking badass okay?! Ladies, you got this.

"

I once crashed into someone's wing mirror and freaked out so much that I drove away in the opposite direction. I then tried to find the car as I felt so bad but they were nowhere to be seen. Sorry if this was you!

"

"

I farted during my first driving lesson because I was so nervous.

"

"

The first time I ever reversed my car I was getting surprise breakfast treats for my boyfriend. He was more surprised by the huge scratch I created on his car.

"

"

Once I got out my friend's car and there was my stale gum that I'd thrown out the window stuck to the side. Definitely left a mark.

"

"

I once scraped the side of my mum's car down a low brick wall. Not badly, but enough to be noticeable. So I definitely just told her I noticed the scrapes and another car must've done it whilst parking next to it sometime and how awful it is that someone didn't stop to leave an apology note or something.

"

"

I drove the side of my mum's car down the side of the big pillars in a multi storey, scratched it going in and reversing out. I text her to say someone had hit the car and drove off, she immediately knew it was me when I pulled up on the drive. I continued with my lie until she said she'd check CCTV and then I confessed. She laughed at me but, fuck me, half the door was caved in.

"

"

I once got caught by an unmarked police car going an average of 99mph, I ended up crying (a lot) and didn't get a ticket - success!

"

"

Learning to drive was a traumatic time for me. I started to learn, then quit after several weeks without taking the test.

After a year or so I tried again, and eventually took the test, but it took me SIX attempts to pass it. On one of the tests I actually had a panic attack (the poor guy only asked me to reverse round a corner!) and it had to be cancelled...

"

"

On a recent journey to my Mum's (about 300 odd miles), it suddenly occurred to me that my car insurance was due, in fact OVERdue, as I was certain it usually automatically renews itself, and I certainly would've seen the payment.

The rest of the journey was made pretty sheepishly, every motorway camera and police car made me wince (I had recently found out about ANPR) and when I arrived I made the relevant phone calls. It turns out I was right, my car was uninsured, which, with pangs of guilt I rectified immediately.

I did some digging about following the call as I was sure it had automatically renewed the year before, dug out the paperwork and statements, and to make matters worse (this is terrible) it turns out, I had been driving UNINSURED FOR A YEAR!?!?!?!!?????

I am an idiot.

(Brownie promise; I am now fully comp)

"

"

I was in a traffic jam, so moving about 0.1 miles an hour every 5 minutes. I somehow still managed to bang into the back of the guy driving in front of me and dented his car. I never admitted I was texting at the time so threw my phone under the car seat as quick as I could so no one noticed. I was also driving my mum's car!

"

"

I was going through a breakup and I used to smoke, one day when I was driving back from an argument with the ex, I flicked my cigarette out the window it dropped into my receipt stash in the door and set fire, I had to pull over and throw a bottle of red wine all over it. Then I got back into the car and drove off, killing a rabbit. It was not a good day.

"

Chapter Nine:

Exercising

(sexing)

I never in a million years thought I'd get my friends to openly talk about this, even anonymously. Exercise mishaps are embarrassing enough; they're often lycra-clad and happening inside a gym that's full of super buff-tings, but to talk about what they get up to in the bedroom? This was, by far, the most answered section of this project. Let's talk about this more in real life, because other than the physical repetition of lifting a fork to my face, sex is about the only form of exercise I get.

My general laziness became so bad at one point, that I invited a very hyper breed of dog into my life. I figured, hey, this will get me out of the house more. This dog was (and still is) way too energetic for me. He's less of a Jack Russell and more of a kangaroo on speed, enjoying his first Christmas, at Disneyland, and is therefore a dog that I avoid as much as possible. I, more wisely, also have a hot-water-bottle breed of Chihuahua, who hates going outside, hates climbing stairs and hates anything that even remotely resembles fruit. We are a match made in heaven.

The main problem I have with exercise, is the fact that the rewards are so far from instant. As in, unreachable. After exercising I feel nothing but sweaty, nauseous, blistery and very grumpy. I look in a mirror afterwards and think, dear Lord, this is definitely much worse than when I started. Without fail, I'm always severely disappointed the next morning, when I discover that I still don't have killer abs despite running almost three kilometres. There goes all motivation. Sex is the exception to this reward rule. Sex instantly cures headaches, releases feel-good endorphins and, in certain positions, has been known to unblock even the most stubborn of blocked sinuses. I'm no doctor, but sex is definitely a cure for most ailments.

There are hundreds and hundreds of women sharing boring yoga tips on their instagram accounts, sharing their 'squat challenge' blogs or new workout routines, and I just think nope. "This is a brand new, guaranteed way to lose weight in six weeks, without leaving your home". Shit, I'd best give you my credit cards details immediately. I know that as someone who struggles to gain weight, I'm in a rare position to not have to find the motivation to exercise, but I'm not sure I'll ever understand what so many of you love about it.

I fully expected this chapter to be one of the shortest and for women to shy away from talking about any kind of nitty gritty here, but I couldn't be happier to have been proven wrong. I'm a firm believer that women should take pride in their healthy appetites for life, whether that's in the kitchen, gym or bedroom. Enjoy.

"

My PE teacher still thinks I have asthma. It's easy to forget your inhaler when you don't have one…

"

"

Whilst training for a half marathon, I found that running sometimes made me need to poo, like, urgently. Thankfully, I never had an accident, but I recall one particular run on a Saturday morning where I'd run a few miles before feeling the need to go. As I had my heart set on running quite a distance that day, I tried to ignore it. But the more I ran, the more it felt like I was going to explode. So I stopped.

That's when I realised I'd run into the middle of nowhere, with no public toilets anywhere. I had no choice but to head back home. I began to take a steady run back, but of course the problem returned. So, I ended up walking to ease the pressure. It was the longest, most uncomfortable walk I have ever had. When I finally reached my house, I flew threw the door as soon as it was unlocked, not even stopping to take off my muddy trainers, as I pegged it to the loo....honestly, I have never felt so relieved.

"

"

I once farted while being supported in a handstand. Not sure who was more embarrassed.

"

"

I once cycled to a client meeting, it had been raining the night before and my bike had been outside. It was only when I arrived at the client's office and got off my bike that I realised the rainwater had soaked into my bike seat, and then soaked into my trousers giving me a gigantic 'I've peed myself' wet patch, which I attempted to cover up in a Mr. Bean-like fashion with my bag.

"

"

I didn't learn how to ride a bike until the ripe age of 25.

"

"

One holiday I wanted to take up bodyboarding, I was starting to get the hang of it. I was halfway out into the sea one day and waiting to catch the right wave. This was it, my moment had finally come, I was in the right position and the timing was perfect, I sat on the board about to lean forwards when the wave snuck up on me.

I caught the wave perfectly but I was still sat up, holding on for dear life, I was going at high speed towards the shore. The wave was powerful and my bikini top flew undone, I could not do anything to save myself as I went hurtling towards a beach full of people with boobs flying everywhere. I landed face down on the shore clutching onto boobs and sorted myself out, how mortifying. Later on in the hotel we were talking to a group of people staying at the same hotel near the beach we were at, talking about how great the sea was, one of the gentlemen in the group said, 'oh yeah, you were the lass, topless, out of control on the body board'.

Kill me now.

"

"

A guy I was seeing once came before we even started the sex part. Not great for the relationship but a huge boost to my confidence in kissing!

"

"

*I'd had litres of wine and vomited on someone's floor
midway through sex. Yes, we carried on.*

"

"

My ex partner went to slap my ass in bed, but instead slapped himself so hard in the testicles we had to stop, but not before I burst out into fits of laughter when he was still inside me.

"

"

I was having sex with my first boyfriend and we both suddenly noticed there was blood. We both (to my horror) assumed my period must've come early or something, until we realised that is was from him and somehow he'd managed to have acquired a little tear that was bleeding like a bloody waterfall. Maybe my vagina was angry at him for some reason, like that film Teeth. Men, beware!

"

"

We all do it, I know we do because it's a scientific thing about air in your fanny (or at least I tell myself that). Queefing. It will always happen if we're doing it doggy style and he pulls my arse cheeks apart! I try hard to hold them in but that backfired on me once and I ended up doing it in his face.

"

"

After gathering myself after a marathon afternoon of
sexytimes, ringing ears and all. I had misheard my then
partner asking me if I was okay, to then myself reply
'did you just say harambe?!' Laughing that hard at the
situation to queef so loud I buried my head under the duvet
in hysterical shame.

"

"

The first time I did it with one guy we lost the condom, we never finished we just laid there totally disheartened. It's something we still talk about to this day and I never had the balls to tell him it was still inside me and I pulled it out when I got home. It was probably there for about an hour.

"

"

I had sex in a bird watching hut at Whisby Nature Park.

"

"

I once pissed myself during foreplay and pretended I'd squirted.

"

"

Myself and my boyfriend at the time were using toys, warming up for anal, it wasn't our first time doing it, but things got very messy …. Never have Mexican food on date night!

"

"

I'd had my nails done, Stiletto Louboutin style (AKA Pointed, sharp.) I was feeling myself and felt sassy, so I got a Butt Plug from Ann Summers.

We got down to it, It was fine, everyone was having a good time, then my partner gasped and said "It's gone".

"What do you mean it's GONE?".

Does a little Looney Tunes hand motion "It just, sucked up, it's inside."

It took me around 15 minutes of panic, lots of pushing, him laughing at me, my housemate texting me asking if I was okay and a very ill-planned thrust of the stiletto nails to get it back out.

On a plus note - I had magic clean poos for 3 months after this. So, there's that.

"

Chapter Ten:

WORKING

(tweeting)

You have the same number of hours in a day that Beyoncé does. Terrifying isn't it? She's taking over the world and all you've done is a Tweet about how much Paul Rudd looks like a young Jason Lee, despite them being the same age.

The average age a woman becomes a mother in the UK is now 34 years old, an all-time high. Why? My guess is that women are either too busy with their careers or, more likely, too busy trying to find one that makes enough money for them to be able to have children at all. Without sounding like an old broken record, previous generations really don't understand how much of a struggle finding work is these days, never mind finding any well-paid work. (FYI, these are the same people that also don't understand the words 'freelance' or 'copywriter', and guess what I do for a living?). It's truly frustrating to live in an age where 16% of people who graduate from university are still unemployed at age 24, but damn it, some bugger from your university class will always make it to the big time. You know the ones, those friends who your mum constantly stalks on Facebook. "Have you seen their latest success story, dear?", "Yes, I did notice that actually, mother, despite multiple attempts to hide their updates from my timeline."

I shouldn't really complain, I am one of the lucky ones. I love writing, I love my freelance team and I love working from wherever I want. If I won the lottery would I do the same thing? Absolutely! The only thing that would change is that I'd bring a few of my other business ideas to life. For example, I think I'd be amazing at writing 'tombstones with a twist', but mourners are notoriously tricky people to market to. In fact, the public in general seem to lack the enthusiasm I have for most of my creative ideas, which is why I stopped tweeting them at Richard Branson.

I really do thank my lucky stars that I don't have a job which means I have to deal with members of the public every day, and trust me, I thank them even harder after reading some of your stories… you are all much better people than I am.

"

I am filling this survey in on work time!

"

"

I am the absolute pinnacle of virtuous femininity and I have definitely never put a client on hold to call them a moron.

"

"

I have wanked in the loo…

"

"

I used to 'forget' to turn the sign to OPEN…

"

"

When I'm desperate for a fart at work, I've always 'conveniently' left something in the car so I can run outside and vent out the gas.

"

"

I've had sex at work after closing time.

"

"

I was once doing a spray tan on this man, it wasn't awkward or uncomfortable, he was really lovely. Half way through I squat down to do his legs and I hear what sounds like a rippling fart. Luckily he was facing away from me so I had a quick check and I'd split my trousers from front to back. I did the whole 'wow it's warm in here' and wrapped my cardigan round my waist stifling my own laughter.

I finished and left the room and told my boss and we were both crying. It wouldn't have been so bad if I wasn't wearing My Little Pony pants. So either he thinks I farted or I'm a total weirdo for laughing in his face when he came out of the treatment room.

Tan was spot on though.

"

"

I've been so tired that I've actually just gone and sat on the loo for a break.

"

"

I once texted (or I guess how the kids say it now - sexted) an image of my boobs to my other half, whilst in the toilet at work - he bloody loved it, and I felt incredibly cheeky and sly for the rest of the day!

"

"

I once had sex at work....there isn't really much more I can say. I literally don't know what I was thinking!

"

"

I was once so hungover at work I was sick in the ice well behind the bar. (It came out of nowhere).

It got emptied and disinfected I promise.

Another job, another bar (I won't mention by name, but a popular vodka bar) ((also I didn't get fired for vomiting in the ice well)), we had monthly time trials and speed tests on our cocktails, but to practise for these without wasting precious alcohol we used empty spirit bottles filled with water. Fast forward an hour after training and someone comes to the bar to complain their shots tasted of water…

To our horror we realised we had never changed the speed rail over, and had been using water instead of spirits for the best part of an hour.

We generously replaced the gents shots who had complained, obviously we didn't say what had happened… whoops.

"

"

I once told a few people that I dated someone who was very popular in the company I worked for. It was completely untrue and I didn't think anyone would believe me, it was ridiculous and I was laughing the entire time. A few months later the rumour was still going around and I had to deny it, even confessing that I made it up. No one believed me, karma at its finest!

"

"

My husband once sent me a rude picture while I was in work, when I opened it unknowingly there was a consultant standing right behind me.

"

"

I wrote an email to my cubicle neighbour about a mutual colleague being a "Fat Bitch who always goes for a shit when we open" and sent it directly to her instead.

"

Thank you

Thank you so much to all of the women who made this possible. Due to the anonymous nature of the survey, it became impossible to know which of you even opened it. All I know is that at least 30 of you filled out at least one section. That's more than half of the women I sent it to, so I was really pleased with that.

I must admit, I tried to guess who a few of you were (in my head), but I was definitely wrong about at least one of you, because you recently apologised for not finding time to fill it out before my deadline. I would never have known.

I'm not going to thank anybody individually, because let's be honest — you'd instantly sue my ass as soon as I sell any movie rights — but a huge thanks to Rox, who was my inspiration for this book. Thank you so much, girl.

And as always, thank you very much for reading.

Huge love, Spadge x